Robert Kennedy III

7 Ways To Know You Were Meant To Lead

First published by LEEP Leadership Media in 2016.

Copyright © Robert Kennedy III, 2016.

All rights reserved. No part of this publication may be reproduced, stored, or transmitted in any form or by any means, electronic, mechanical, photocopying, recording, scanning, or otherwise without written permission from the publisher. It is illegal to copy this book, post it to a website, or distribute it by any others means without permission.

First Edition.

ISBN: 978-1537312965

This book was professionally typeset on Reedsy.
Find out more at reedsy.com

Contents

Dedication	i
Praise For 7 Ways	ii
Introduction	v
Way #1 - Leaders Are Courageous	1
Way #2 - Leaders Are Creative	6
Way #3 - Leaders Choose Results Over Credit	10
Way #4 - Leaders Know They Need People	14
Way #5 - Leaders Just Show Up	19
Way #6 - Leaders Believe Even If Everyone Else Doesn't	24
Way #7 - Leaders Are Undaunted By Failure	33
What's Your Label?	38
What Happens Next?	44
Acknowledgments	47
About The Author	49
Broken Rules	50

Dedication

First, I'm learning every day what it means to love because I'm learning about the God who loves me. To my Lord and Savior.

Second, every book I write is going to be dedicated to my wife, Nadia Kennedy, because she allows me to be who I am in spite of the challenges that provides.

Third, I also want to dedicate this to my "GramPah", Robert I, who shows us with every passing moment what it means to have lifelong swagger!

Last but not least, Dad & Mom, I'm just barely beginning to understand your sacrifice. Thank you. I love you.

Praise For 7 Ways

"Be ready to be challenged on your conventional beliefs about leadership. In 7 Ways To Know You Were Meant To Lead, Robert Kennedy III busts common leadership myths and explores what it means to be a modern day leader both at work and in life." – ***Kevin Kruse, New York Times Bestselling Author Employee Engagement 2.0***

I love this book, it's simple, pragmatic and inspiring. With this book Robert demystifies leadership and makes it accessible to everyone. He makes you believe you can lead…and everyone who has dreamed of being a leader should read this book as it will help you achieve that goal. Fully recommended!!! – ***Gordon Tredgold, author, 4 Principles Every Business Needs to Achieve Success and Drive Results, Inc Magazine Top 100 Leadership Expert and Speaker***

Robert is the perfect person to write about leadership. Not only is he a clear and strategic thinker, he also walks his talk. You can trust the advice in 7 Ways to Know You Were Meant to Lead. By following it, you will watch your impact soar."–***Pamela Slim, author, Body of Work and Escape from Cubicle Nation***

The path of leadership can be winding and difficult to navigate. Leaders can often find themselves at a point where they are questioning whether they were meant to lead. Robert, in his usual down-to-earth, practical style, gives leaders seven points of evaluation to move them towards clarity and help them succeed as a leader. This book is a must-read for every leader who wants to get better and take their leadership to the next level. When a leader is clear about their purpose and place in leadership, they are freed to lead like never before – and Robert's book will position you to get there! - ***Tim Parsons, writer, Leadership for the Rest of Us***

Get. This. Book. In Robert Kennedy III's latest book he outlines seven ways you know you were meant to lead. Even better, he tells you **how** to embrace leadership opportunities around you – in your family, in your community, with friends, and with work colleagues.

Robert offers relevant examples and stories from children, team members, sports stars, and fellow musicians. His wide range of experiences help the reader understand how widely varying the opportunities for leadership are.

And, he inspires the reader to engage in those leadership opportunities.

Our world needs inspiring leaders – and this book is just the ticket to start your journey to being one. - ***S. Chris Edmonds Speaker, Consultant, Author of The Culture Engine***

Robert Kennedy's writing style is authentic and real. He strikes the perfect mix between inspiration and practical advice. In this book, he hits the ball out of the park as an expert on the core aspects and makeup of a true leader. If you want to know whether you were meant to lead, and while you are at it connect with your authentic self while learning how you can best help others, buy this book and read it." - ***Jeff Davis,*** *author of Reach Your Mountaintop: 10 Keys to Finding the Hidden Opportunity in Your Setbacks, Flipping What You've Heard On Its Head, and Achieving Legendary Goals.*

Robert, I have completed your book, and I absolutely complement you on the great job you did in writing it. It is an impactful message, and it is very easy to read due to the excellent job of weaving in your personal stories to share the message. My biggest takeaways from the book are a clear understanding that leadership has nothing to do with a "Title". God created us to lead through serving others and your 7 ways to know you are a leader point out that fact. However, a person cannot sit on those gifts and skills, instead they need to put them into action to lead and serve others. Awesome!!

Here is my endorsement:
"In his book, 7 *Ways to Know That You Were Meant to Lead*, Robert Kennedy III debunks the myth that leaders are only those with a high profile title. He provides 7 keys attributes of leadership that you can take action upon and step into making a positive difference within your sphere of influence. You will enhance your leadership impact by reading this book!" - ***Mark Deterding, Executive Coach, Author of Leadership, Jesus' Way***

Introduction

Were you born to lead or is it something that you had to learn? Are there people who are born to lead and others who were simply made to…well…follow? If you were born to follow, is that an insult or does that mean you are less than the person who was born to lead? What about leaders…must they lead all the time? Is that their lot? Do they HAVE to even if they don't feel like it?

If you are anything like me, you've asked those questions and even more. For as long as I can remember, the word "leadership" has been somewhere around me. It's either been applied to me, someone else around me or given as an aspiration. Leadership was a good thing and that's just what my family was bred to be…leaders. Having the last name "Kennedy" didn't help dispel that notion at all. There wasn't an application. There was no survey. There was no question. You're a Kennedy, you lead. That is all. I had the historical/political landscape which created that expectation. However, this didn't exist for my grandfather. He was around before JFK, RFK, MLK and all of the 3 initial K's. My grandfather, Robert Kennedy, (who happens to be 102 and rockin' it as of this writing) knew that he had to lead. His mindset was first that of a man and a father. He had to provide for his family but he also had to create a way. In leading, he had to sometimes leave his family to travel internationally for work. But, his message remained consistent. Trust God, fulfill your responsibilities and don't be afraid to take the step FIRST!

Taking the step FIRST and taking the FIRST step are a bit different. Leaders do both. They operate in a manner which says "this needs to be done whether anyone follows or not." They push forward to progress whether it makes sense or not. They simply decide they will...LEAD!

Many have misconceptions about leadership and knowing whether or not they qualify. Some of those myths include:

- Leaders are born
- You must have a title to lead
- Others must recognize you as a leader first
- You are always either a leader or a follower
- You must be a leader from a young age

This book will dispel some of the myths and help you to understand how you may already be leading. You'll then be able to step into your true mantle of leadership. As you go through, take the time to answer the questions provided so that you can take inventory of your beliefs and actions. This introspection is a necessary step in personal growth and leadership development. In fact, the reason many leaders fail is because of an unwillingness to take personal inventory and seek feedback. Some leaders fail without even knowing they are failing. They make the assumption that as long as the organization is "alive", they must be doing fine.

But, they miss the point. "Fine" is not acceptable for leaders.

A leader must seek greatness and never settle for just simply reaching a flat place on the mountain climb. A leader must not only check themselves. They should also intentionally invite opportunities for receiving external feedback without being offended. This is the vulnerability needed to create trust. But, I'll get around to writing that book at another time.

Let's clarify one more thing. When we talk about leaders, you might think I am only talking about organizational leaders...CEOs, Presidents, Pastors, Directors, Principals. But, leaders can be found in many spaces. In fact, you might simply find one looking back at you in the mirror.

Let's take a look at you and 7 Ways To Know You Were Meant To Lead.

1

Way #1 - Leaders Are Courageous

The difference between leaders and the average person is leaders are courageous. By courage, some might think I mean "without fear." Some might think I am talking about a warrior who is fearlessly bold, who has no qualms about moving forward into the heat of battle, without worrying about the possible results. But that's just not true. Leaders have fears just like everyone else. The difference is they choose not to let fear dictate how they proceed. They choose to move forward in spite of how they feel. They choose to take action despite their emotions. They decide they will not allow external, or even internal, factors to deter them from progress.

Does this occur naturally? Maybe. I'm not 100% sure. But there does seem to be a group of people who are willing to move forward in spite of what people are saying or how things may seem. This is not just an adult phenomenon. It even happens in children.

Have you ever watched a group of children playing? Were you able to pick out a child from the group or maybe an entire group of children willing to move forward fearlessly? Well, at least it seems fearless. One of my children, as I watch him play with his friends, it seems as if he moves forward without fear. He jumps on the monkey bars and moves about as if the metal can never hurt him. He may sit observing other children playing and if he chooses to join in, then he does. He does this with little observable emotion. He may decide he will give the instructions and lead the charge. Then at other times, he may sit, seemingly detached yet keenly taking in everything that is going on. Is he fearless? Of course not.

During our first trip to Disney World, we decided we would go on a roller coaster. We waited in line for about 45 minutes. As we made it up to the front of the line, he calmly let us know he did not want to ride the coaster. For a minute, I was bothered and frustrated as my mind created all sorts of questions, wondering why he had let us wait so long before deciding he didn't want to ride this coaster. He was scared. But the amazing part of me was his demeanor. He calmly said, "I don't want to go on this one. I'm a little frightened."

"I don't want to fight you."

He didn't shake. He didn't quiver. He didn't cry. He didn't cling to my leg. He simply stated, "I don't want to go on this one. I'm a little frightened."

In reflecting on it, I realized there was courage in not being concerned about the frustration he must have known we would feel. Should you ignore the feelings of others in order to satisfy your own desires? No. That would be a horrible blanket statement. But, I had to admit in this circumstance, the dichotomy of calmly stating your feeling and that feeling being one of fear struck me. I had to smile at the courage of a child to acknowledge what he was feeling but yet state it in such a collected manner.

Some might say "true courage" would have been to be frightened and do it anyway. But, I saw courage in sizing up the situation and knowing what he wanted to do. It's the same as the child who, when confronted by a charging, instigating bully, simply continues walking, focusing on the path ahead and says, "I don't want to fight you."

That too is courage!

Parents often try to control children with fear. I remember when one of my children (yes, this same child as above) decided he didn't want to eat dinner. There was something on his plate which he didn't particularly like and he decided he was just not going to touch it. One of the "motivators" we used at the time (right or wrong) was dessert. We told our son that if he didn't eat the meal in front of him, he would get no dessert. He sat there for a few moments and looked up as if he was thinking about his options.

"Hmmmm, ok. I think I'll just not have dessert."

He then simply excused himself and went to bed. WOW! My wife and I hadn't even considered the possibility he could or would choose the option so many kids seem to be afraid of. Some people are just like that. They decide to move forward despite what is happening around them. They may not be able to access the same "rewards" as everyone else. But, they have an ability to create an internal reward. It might simply be the joy of knowing they chose to do it their own way.

Leadership guru, John Maxwell, notes, "Successful leaders have the courage to take action when others choose to hesitate." That action may not be the anticipated or expected action. But, there is courage in taking action against the grain or different from what others expect, even in the face of disagreeable response and emotion.

As a parent and a leader, I would much rather grow a leader who isn't afraid of making the courageous choice instead of simply tackling what everyone else expects in the way they expect it.

Let's look at you.

Discovery Questions

1. What do you think defines courage?

2. When confronted with the possibility of upsetting people, how do you normally proceed?

3. Who in your life would you consider courageous? Why?

4. What is the most courageous thing you have ever done?

2

Way #2 - Leaders Are Creative

Creativity is reserved for artists...right? We're led to think this because colors, fashion, dance and the arts are what society tends to label as creative. Every so often, we will hear about someone who was a creative problem solver. But, in our education systems, the word "creative" is attached to arts...as in the "creative arts" program. Outside of the arts, everything else is a logical system and process that just fits together like a glove and makes sense. At least, it's made to seem that way.

The truth is creativity is all around us and we need not look far for it's in all of us. However, creativity requires something we usually don't hear about. Creativity requires courage.

"Creativity requires courage"

I remember working on my first musical project with a singing group. We were in the studio and I was in a space where I was constantly writing new music. I was writing and teaching a new song at almost every rehearsal. We were performing some of them live and enjoying the process. However, it wasn't until we met with a producer for the first time that I realized the courage inside of creativity. We took in several songs to the producer and he listened to what I thought was one of my best songs at the time. I was so proud of the lyrics, the transitions and the key changes. He listened for 5 minutes and told us the song should be 2 or 3 separate songs. He wanted to break the song apart.

WHAT?

I felt like I had just been shot in the chest. The song was my baby and I had given birth to it. Now, he was telling me it needed to be torn apart. Many of the songs came from a place of spiritual experience and were essentially me pouring out my feelings to God at the time. Now, those feelings would be on display. Up until that point, I'd had my head down writing. The producer's critical response made me realize these songs, these inner parts of me were going to be accessible to other people and they could respond to them in a way that I might not like or agree with. In fact, since we had already sung some of them, people were already responding to them.

But, what if I had chosen just to write them and never share them? It's like the age old question, "If a tree falls in a forest and no one is there, does it make a sound?"

If I have creative thoughts or ideas but never choose to courageously act on them, am I really identified as creative? The answer is no. You are simply a closet dreamer. The moment you decide to publicly ACT on an inspiration, you become a leader. The minute you choose to pursue a creative option, one which might make no sense to others, you become a leader.

As much as we don't like problems, it's precisely at the moment problems occur when the true jewel of creativity shows up. This is when the innovative leaders shine. They look at the problem, turn it on its side and then create a plan of attack steering away from the norm. If they don't have a workable approach, they search for someone who does.

Kevin Plank was a fullback playing football for the University of Maryland. After his practices and games, he would change out of his t-shirt which was soaked through with perspiration. The soaked t-shirt stuck to his body underneath his jersey and he found this annoying. However, he noted that the compression shorts he wore under his pants stayed fairly dry. This gave him an idea to make a t-shirt using similar synthetic fabric. Once he developed the prototype, he gave some to some of his friends who had moved up to play in the NFL. UnderArmour was born.

This may seem to be a simple story about an entrepreneur. But, ask this question: If t-shirts had gotten sweaty and sticky prior to Kevin, what happened to all of the other people who it annoyed?

You might even wonder why compression shorts of the appropriate material existed at the time but no one had thought to apply the properties to t-shirts. Kevin saw a problem and decided to apply a little creativity to come up with a solution.

Then he shared his creative solution with others.

You might know the rest of the story. UnderArmour is a 10 year old, multi-billion dollar company that continues to grow despite being in a market with giants 7 or 8 times its age.

Let's look at you.

Discovery Questions

1. *What problems have you solved creatively?*

2. *Do you tend to go with the status quo or do you drive towards a solution?*

3. *Do you tend to seek out challenges or do you look for the smoothest path to success?*

3

Way #3 - Leaders Choose Results Over Credit

Harry S. Truman is credited with the quote, "It's amazing what you can accomplish when you don't care who gets the credit."

Leaders often get the credit when things go well. During the years when it seemed like the US economy was on the rebound, the stock market and the real estate market were flying high, Bill Clinton got a lot of credit for his leadership. Outside of the scandal elements, which we won't address here, his presidency was looked at as one of the most successful in recent history. In fact, if a third term were allowed, many polls indicated Bill Clinton would have been re-elected. But, did Clinton actually do everything himself to cause the country to "prosper"? If you know anything about Congress and the Senate, then the easy answer is no. BUT, he did get the credit.

Leaders also get the blame when things don't go so well. But, some tend to sidestep the blame and look for scapegoats when the blame begins to be passed around. I remember being the director for a division in a health organization. I had approximately 20 staff and 3 supervisors in my department. In this particular industry, there was terrible turnover and the stress level was high. This often meant keeping staff morale up was a major chore. I had one particular supervisor who had been elevated to supervisor but I'm not so sure she wanted to be there. She was a very hard worker but motivating or coordinating her team was just not something she found enjoyable.

One of the responsibilities of our team was medication deliveries to our community clients. This was a critical part of the job and it couldn't be ignored. However, there were several times when there was a such a breakdown, I ended up having to go out in the evening to take care of this task. When I asked this supervisor about the breakdown, her response was typically, "I had my kids and I couldn't leave," or "John/Mary said they would do it but they didn't," or "The schedule was messed up and we didn't know that our team was on for delivery." The closest she ever came to "I" was when she mentioned her kids.

Her responses were not ridiculous. But they never addressed how she would handle the problem going forward nor did they ever indicate responsibility. However, as director for the division, I had to take the responsibility. If I were to report to my VP that my staff failed, her response to me would be, "well, then YOU failed!"

This is the tough part of leadership. You get credit when you win and must take responsibility when you lose. The trouble for some industries is there is a lot more losing than winning. This can take its toll.

But, what if the leader were less concerned about credit and simply looked for ways to create a result?

"Leaders have a goal and see a destination. Then, they do what it takes to get there."

I was elected president of my Toastmasters club in Maryland. If you have never heard of Toastmasters, it's a public speaking and leadership organization. There are more than 15,000 clubs worldwide with more than 300,000 members. In each election year, there is a list of 10 goals that clubs may strive for. If you reach 5 of the goals, you are noted as a **Distinguished** club. If the club reaches 7, they are listed as **Select Distinguished** and at 9 goals, **President's Distinguished**.

Since our club had been in existence only a little more than 1 year, it had not reached the goal of Distinguished as yet. My goal was to get our club to Distinguished no matter what it took. Our team of officers took on the task of identifying the goals it would take for us to reach distinguished. Then, we went to work. Throughout the year, I began to notice a little less engagement from some of the officers, many due to their work schedule. This was a volunteer position for all of us and some had work begin to take over a bit. They were unable to complete some of their responsibilities. This resulted in our club missing out on 2 of the goals that we agreed on. Some evaluation was now required and we determined where we would need to adjust. In order to reach the goal, we would need to strive for some of the more challenging goals and motivate people in the club to push a bit harder.

As the leader, I took on the challenge of accomplishing 3 of the goals and was able to help 2 other club members reach goals as well. My focus in this was getting to the goal of Distinguished club. This was the goal and this was where we HAD to reach. We were able to submit our last goal with 2 weeks left in our calendar year.

Now, don't get me wrong. I did receive some awards for completing the goals I set out to achieve. But the focus was not on me. It was on getting to a specific result. I simply realized the best way for me to get our club to an achievement we desired was to get on the achievement train myself. Not only did I need to get on the train, I also needed to set the pace.

Leaders have a goal and see a destination. They do what it takes to get there whether they get recognized for it or not.

Let's look at you.

Discovery Questions

1. Think about a time when you have completed a project but were not given any accolades for it. When was it and what did it include?

2. How did you feel about it?

3. Is progress or praise more important to you?

4

Way #4 - Leaders Know They Need People

"No man is an island...no man stands alone"

I confess. Sometimes I've got Superman Syndrome. It's a dangerous disease and it's widespread. I see the dreams and the ideas and I often attempt to accomplish them with my own strength, my own resources, and my own willpower. Most of the time, it's not that successful. I need people and I constantly have to remind myself about it. I know it in my heart but it's not always easy to put in practice. Why?

People are complex. People are tough to figure out. People need to be inspired, empowered and motivated. That can get tiring, right?

"...if you can do it yourself, then the idea isn't big enough."

John Maxwell refers to leadership with a one word definition...influence. Nothing more, nothing less. To lead people, you must first get them to buy into you, then to buy into themselves and finally to buy into an idea worth doing. If an idea is big enough, then it absolutely needs people. In fact, if you can do it yourself, then the idea isn't big enough. This is not to say only leaders can have big ideas. It's not to say you must have a big idea in order to be a leader either. In fact, many leaders don't have big ideas. They just have the drive to get things done.

In his book, *Drive*, Daniel Pink tells the story of William McKnight, the CEO of 3M. McKnight simply believed in the mantra, "hire good people and leave them alone." He wrote *"Management that is destructively critical when mistakes are made kills initiative. And it's essential that we have many people with initiative if we are to continue to grow."*

McKnight put this to the test by allowing technical employees to allocate up to 15% of their time on projects of their choosing. It was during some of this "free time" that one of the scientists, Spencer Silver, came up with the idea for what would later become Post-It notes. McKnight knew while he was seen as the person at the head of the line, the great innovations and ideas came about because he allowed people to exercise their creative minds. The challenge with creative minds can be keeping them locked in on the process. Managing a multiplicity of creative minds can be a joy and a nightmare. As a creative mind myself,

I have experienced the euphoria of a brilliant revelation and also a brainstorm session where everyone is energized by the onslaught of ideas. I've also seen what can happen when there are a lot of ideas but no one to focus the ideas.

Leaders need people, but they also need the RIGHT people.

I was once a part of a potential music project where writers and musicians came together to play music they had written, share ideas they had and discuss new ones. The ages in the room ranged from 16 to 45. The vibe in the room was amazing. Everyone was excited about the creative juices flowing and sharing ideas they had pent up inside. We played some recordings; I hopped on to the keyboard and played a couple of my ideas; others simply sang what was in their hearts. There were a couple of young people with an idea and they got excited about it. Soon, they excused themselves to another room for about 30 minutes before coming back and presenting us with the idea. They sang and everyone cheered them on because of their creativity. The room was full of creative minds or people who wanted to be creative. It was amazing!

After we left the room, each of us went back to our homes, our studios, our minds, our lives. We went back to doing what we were doing because everyone in the room was playing the role of a creator but no one was an organizer in the effort...well, at least no one TOOK that role. The project died and we never so much as spoke about the day again. Great music. Great ideas. But, individual creativity ruled!

Leaders not only need people, but they need different types of

people. Some leaders know this instinctively and some know it via trial and error. But, they know whatever is happening doesn't happen unless they seek out a team who can play the right roles to win. No one understands this more than athletes in team sports like basketball.

LeBron James is seen as arguably the best all-around athlete the NBA has ever seen. He has led his teams, at this writing, to 3 NBA Championships and is widely known to be the leader of the teams on which he plays. As great players often do, he can be known to simply dominate and take over a game. However, in the early stages of his career, this ability did not win him any championships. He was strong enough, fast enough, and talented enough to get his team, the Cleveland Cavaliers, to the NBA Finals a couple of times but was unable to get them over the hump on his own. He decided to "take his talents" to South Beach Miami to join with some other players who were excellent in their roles. They were leaders in their own right and had even won with other players. But, this collaboration was going to be effective because they were all excellent at different positions. They were all elite in their own areas. While talented enough, if everyone played the same position LeBron played, it wouldn't have worked out in the same way. They needed the different roles and no doubt, they needed each other in order to win the championship.

Many are kept from true success because they attempt everything on their own and often choose NOT to allow anyone on their team. Others are blocked because they choose allow ANYONE on their team. Leaders need people but they also know they need people with different abilities, who play different roles and positions. This is a leadership formula for success.

Let's look at you.

Discovery Questions

1. *Do you prefer to work on your own or are you naturally inclined to include people?*

2. *Do you simply prefer to work with your friends or do you seek the best people who can fit the roles necessary for success?*

3. *Do people expect you to lead?*

5

Way #5 - Leaders Just Show Up

When I was a kid, we would sometimes have to go to meetings at church with my dad at different times during the week. Dad would tell us that he had to get to church by 5:30 PM. So, we would get ready, hop in the car and go. Most of the time, when we arrived, no one else was there. We were the first ones. We would get there and wait quite some time before anyone showed up. In the meantime, Dad was in his office or in another part of the meeting area preparing himself. My child-mind often wondered why we were the first ones and why we had to wait for others. I asked Dad about it one day. Without looking up from what he was writing, he simply responded, "Leaders show up first."

By contrast, I've had some experiences where the flip took place. I would arrive at meetings, rehearsals and events where the one who was in charge came rushing in 10-15 minutes after the proposed time. Without fail, they always looked disheveled and out of sorts. They would quickly shuffle to the podium out of breath and the first thing they did was apologize. If this happened once, it would be understandable, but these "leaders" seemed to be always running behind.

I was leading a meeting once which I started about 4 minutes late. I was there on time. However, I decided that I would wait for a few more people to show up. There were 3 people out of 8 expected and by the time we began, 2 more arrived. We had the meeting and because some were late, we went over about 10 minutes. One of the leaders in this group, who was on time, pulled me to the side and quite nicely gave me some feedback. She said, "When we start and end things at the time we say that we were going to, it builds trust." Then she left. *Ain't* that something? You get feedback dropped in your lap and the person just spins and leaves. It was her way of saying, 'here-you-go-now-you-decide-what-to-do-with-it'.

I never forgot it. When you lead, people are looking at your words as well as your actions. They dissect and observe your actions not just once, but over a period of time. This is the consistency check. They do so because they want to know if they can depend on you, lean on you...TRUST you. Trust is integral to any project because of the risk factor. If the leader suggests something risky, the team wants to know they can follow because the leader is *all-in* and will have their back should any slip-ups occur.

"I had accepted the responsibility and so I needed to show up."

In Chapter 3, I mentioned the health organization for which I worked. There were quite a few challenging situations where

WAY #5 - LEADERS JUST SHOW UP

I had to SHOW UP even when I didn't want to. One of the responsibilities of my division was to make sure that our clients in the community had the correct medication and dosages for the day, or the proper frequency required. One evening, after a particularly busy day at work, I came in expecting to enjoy my time in front of the TV. Snow had begun to fall that afternoon and of course, we were in for a pretty good sized helping of the white stuff. I cooked dinner, then sat down to eat and "veg" before turning in to sleep. It was now about 6:30pm. I ate and watched a show or two before receiving a call at 7:30 to let me know the person who was assigned to deliver the medications was stuck and couldn't do it. I could feel my blood pressure rising a bit as I began to realize my plans to enjoy a relaxing evening were just about to be derailed. Getting my phone list, I began to make some calls to some of the other staff who I thought were dependable. After making 3 or 4 unsuccessful calls, it began to slowly dawn on me that I was going to have to go out in the snow in order to make this happen. Truth be told, I could have done this immediately upon receiving the news, but somewhere in the back of my mind, I had the idea that I shouldn't be doing it because it was the job of the staff and I was the "director". I never said this out loud but looking back, I realize that I definitely did think it. In hindsight, it is very possible it might have come out in my body language. I trudged out into the snow, started up my car and made the slow trek to the office.

When I got there, I walked in and turned on the lights. The feeling I got then wasn't one of frustration, but instead one of loneliness. At that moment, I felt very alone as a leader. I felt forced into doing something I really didn't want to do. I felt like my staff had let me down. I felt like the weather had set me up. I felt like I was standing in the middle of a room yelling, the intense interrogation light trained on me and no one could hear me. But, the truth was, I had accepted the responsibility and I needed to show up. So, I sat, took a breath, got out the lists, grabbed the medications I needed and made the slow journey out into the storm. Two and a half hours later, I made it back into the office, tired, drained but proud I was able to complete the job, meet our clients needs and save my team from any embarrassment or harassment.

Leadership is rarely about what you WANT to do. It is mostly about what MUST be done! That "must" may come from the vision set by you or it may come from circumstances beyond your control. In either case, the leader must still SHOW UP if he or she wants to get the result they desire. They must SHOW UP if they want to be able to pull their team along with them to victory. They must SHOW UP so their actions are always in sync with their words. When they are out of sync, it can be very difficult to gain trust and momentum. They SHOW UP even when they feel all alone because even more important than feeling good is leaving a legacy of perseverance and "no-quit" attitude.

Let's look at you.

Discovery Questions

1. *What was one circumstance where you knew something had to*

be done but felt like you were left all alone to do it?

2. How did it turn out?

3. Do you normally show up early, on time or are you typically rushing and late?

4. With regard to time, how much margin for error do you typically give yourself?

6

Way #6 - Leaders Believe Even If Everyone Else Doesn't

They told him that if he went too far, his boat would simply fall over the edge of the world.

They said the human body couldn't sustain the exertion required to complete a mile in 4 minutes. Blood vessels would burst and the heart would just give out.

They said he couldn't be president because the nation wouldn't accept his heritage.

I can vouch for the third statement above because it happened during my lifetime. The first two are stories I've heard in school and in conversation. Since hearing them, I've done some research and it appears there are elements of exaggeration in them. Despite the hyperbole, the aspect of how a leader's mind works and perceives necessary action is still true. There are people who discourage and play down a leader's ideas. The leader must be strong enough to believe.

There is something special about people who are able to stand up and push forward in the face of what everyone else says is impossible. It takes a special ability to hear denigrating statements and yet use them simply as fuel. Michael Jordan attributed his "killer instinct" on the basketball court to his ability to use every NO and every dismissive statement he had heard as fuel for his greatness. This "fuel" is something great leaders rely on and yet it's something most people don't understand. In the moment, as it is taking place, the do-er is thought to be crazy or insane. They are dismissed and often called names. They are even told they are not dealing in reality. How many times have you heard THAT phrase uttered?

For years, there was a teaching or belief the earth was flat. Many years before Ferdinand Magellan sailed, this idea was dispelled. He was a well studied naval explorer and knew there was a way to reach the Spice Islands by circumnavigating the globe. Even with this knowledge, there was still no evidence it had been accomplished before. In order to achieve this, he would need to get a crew together. Here's the challenge with leadership. Even when the leader believes, he/she still needs to convince others to believe also. They don't need to believe in the possibility. They simply need to believe in the leader. The leader's belief must be visible and passionate. This energetic passion creates the fire which sparks the belief in others. His belief led him to leave Spain with 3 ships and 270 crew members in 1519. They followed the path they had planned with many challenges and obstacles. They lost ships along the way. Think about this. It was a trip never taken before and many knew they might not return from this trip. Magellan's belief had to be palpable enough for the crew members to say yes to their own deaths and sacrifice. Magellan died in battle in 1521 and would never complete the actual trip. But, his translator, co-navigator and slave, Enrique was one of the 18 crew members who returned to Spain 3 years later. Magellan is credited in our history books with being the first to make a worldwide trip. But, he actually didn't complete the trip. *He simply believed it could be done.*

Roger Bannister competed in the 1952 Olympics, running in the 1500 meters. He finished fourth in this race. But, it marked a turning point for him. This moment lit a fire in him to become the first to complete a sub-4 minute mile. Others were gunning for this title but he was determined to get it. Now, how could someone who finished fourth in a race be the first to get to a milestone even faster than the person who won? Between 1953 and 1954, other athletes, in particular, John Landy of Australia, ran the mile in increasingly lower times, with Landy getting as low as 4:02.4 in April of that year. Roger hadn't done nearly as much competitive running since the Olympics as others, partly because he was also studying to be a doctor. If sporting events of today are any indication, the people who surround an athlete, who know their training regimen well, can tell you how well an athlete will do at any upcoming event in comparison with others. For example, in 1990, members of Mike Tyson's training team knew he was not as prepared entering his fight with James "Buster" Douglas. The result? Tyson, one of the most vicious punchers of the 80's, suffered his first loss by devastating knockout. So, I can only imagine what was happening around Bannister in 1953 and 1954. He was being told he wasn't doing enough. But, he believed two things. He believed he needed to prioritize studying for his medical degree. He also believed he could beat the 4 minute mile. When Landy ran his 4:02 in April, Bannister knew it would be Landy's last attempt for at least a few months. He knew he had to act at that point. He took part in a meet on May 6, 1954. After running his last lap in 59 seconds, it was announced to enormous cheers, he had finished the race in 3 minutes and 59 seconds. He believed he could do it and more importantly, he ACTED at the right time. Less than 2 months later, Landy achieved a time of 3:57. But, he missed his place in the record books because of the importance of the 4 minute barrier.

Barack Obama was born to a mother from Wichita, Kansas and a father from Kenya...mixed parentage. Based on the accepted system of classification in the US, he is listed as African-American. (My thoughts about this system are for another book). While at Harvard Law School, he was elected the first African-American president of the Harvard Law Review. This gained national attention and served as the catalyst for his first book. In 1992, while in Chicago, he led over 700 volunteers in a voter registration campaign known as Project Vote. They were able to achieve their stated goal of registering more than 150,000 of 400,000 unregistered African American voters in the area. This notoriety led to several different legal appointments up to his election as State Senator of Illinois in 1996. He continued to grow and his name continued to be shared in political circles with him eventually announcing his candidacy for president of the United States in 2006. Since there had never been an acknowledged African-American president of the United States in 43 tries, it was doubtful he would be able to move the needle this time around. The closest an African-

American had come was Jesse Jackson's ill-fated bid for the Democratic nomination in the 1980's. Many thought it was an impossible task. But, Barack believed...moving the nation with his rally call, "Yes, We Can!" A man with less than a decade in politics, called "unseasoned" by many, who didn't have the financial lineage of many of his predecessors, pulled off the improbable by simply starting with the belief that "Yes, He Could!"

Growing up, I heard that there were 3 types of people:

Pessimists: those who always believed the worst was going to happen

Optimists: those who always believed the best could happen

Realists: those who use facts and past events to predict what will happen

The pessimists were painted as being negative. The optimists were painted as being dreamers who ignored reality. The realists were said to be grounded people who lived in the world as it was presented to them. The implied meaning for me was that a pessimist always assumed failure in any risk; the optimist always assumed success in any risk; and, a realist never took a risk unless they had evidence it would pay off.

But, sometimes, there really is no exact evidence that it will pay off. Sometimes, it really is just that...a blind faith risk. And yet, when it pays off, it is no longer thought of as impossible. Someone has to have the unshakeable belief that there is a possibility of winning. Someone has to have the unwavering faith that there is something phenomenal behind the curtain. Someone must possess the guts in order to get to the glory. This calls for the type of belief that moves forward when everyone else is laughing and saying no. This is the mantra of a leader…Belief.

For leaders, this belief is not only in impossible things. Belief extends to people. There are times when no one has belief in a particular person on a team or the person may not even believe in themselves. I remember being in college and watching some of the basketball players in the gym challenging each other to their own little dunk contests. At this stage, they were just trying to see who could dunk the ball at all. None of them were super tall. If memory serves me, the tallest of the group might have been about 6'4". But most averaged 6 feet to 6'1". They would all go back and forth, attempting dunks…some making, some missing, but they were all having a good time laughing with each other. During one particular contest, a student came into the gym who was a bit shorter than these others…about 5'9". As they were playing around, they could see that he was fairly quick and could hold his own. But, when they lined up to start dunking, he got in the line as well. You could see some of them beginning to look at each other as if to say, "what's this little dude trying to do?"

They began taking turns, running toward the basket, ball in hand, then giving a tremendous hop right before the basket that would hopefully propel them far enough to dunk the ball. As normally happened, some made it on the first attempt and some didn't. But, everyone seemed to really pay attention when it was the shorter player's turn. He took the same running start as everyone else, grabbed the ball with 2 hands, then eyed his take-off point. As he took off, he cocked back his right arm and slammed the ball through the hoop. The audible gasps started flying around the gym as most couldn't believe what they just saw. Some immediately said, "Yo, do that again!"

"Leaders believe in possibility."

They couldn't believe what they had just seen. In fact, if they had to choose a dunk team prior to this, he wouldn't have been chosen simply because no one would have believed he had the height or the "hops" to make it. However, when he was asked how he was able to do it, he simply responded, "Coz I believe I can do it."

There was a self-belief that was evident and some even said he believed because he had done it before. Their argument was he wouldn't believe if he never dunked before. But, the opposite is true. He dunked because he believed if he worked hard enough, he could. I highly doubt he was able to dunk on his very first effort. That's just not how it works. People see challenges and attempt them. They usually fail on their first attempt. But, there is something internal, something strong, something focused, which keeps them moving forward. It's belief.

Leaders not only believe in themselves. They believe in others. They believe so much in people that people believe in themselves as a result. John Maxwell refers to this as "putting a 10 above their heads." When he meets people for the very first time, he puts a "10" above their heads in his mind, meaning he thinks they have maximum potential. When you think this about someone, it comes through in how you interact with them. People sense your belief in them and respond to that belief. This sense of connection comes through as "belief energy". This connection is felt palpably because it's unique. Most people don't have people who automatically believe in them and so it makes sense when most don't believe in themselves. There is an energy and strength in belief. Great leaders seem to understand this.

Belief in things, belief in themselves and belief in people; leaders believe even if everyone else doesn't. While considering facts, leaders optimistically believe in possibility. And sometimes, their belief is so strong, myths are created to make for an even better story.

Let's look at you.

Discovery Questions

1. Reflect on a time when you were sure that you were right about something but everyone else thought you were nuts. What did you end up doing?

2. When you believe in something, how strongly do you defend your position? Why?

3. Has there been a time when you set off to do something on your own simply because no one else would buy in? Why did you do that?

7

Way #7 - Leaders Are Undaunted By Failure

Ten year old Walter got up every morning at 4:30 to deliver newspapers with his brother. Then in the evening, he would do another round of deliveries for another newspaper company. Because of this exhausting schedule, he often fell asleep during his classes at school. As a result, he had poor grades. But, his interest really wasn't in school. It was in cartooning. He drew cartoons wherever he could and whenever he could. He took Saturday courses and even a correspondence course in cartooning. During high school, he served as cartoonist for his high school paper while also taking night classes at the Chicago School of Fine Arts.

After leaving high school, he spent some time as an ambulance driver for the Army. He would often draw cartoons on the side of his ambulance as decoration. Upon leaving the army, he was hired as a cartoonist at a Kansas City newspaper. He would work here for a short time but the editor would later fire him telling him that his work "lacked imagination and was not creative enough".

Walter would go on to start and acquire several companies, including one known as Laugh-O-Gram, which all ended in failure and bankruptcy. However, his belief in his work was so strong that he decided to move to California to start an animation studio with his brother called the Disney Brothers Studio. You know the rest of the story. Mickey was born and Walt Disney created one of the most successful companies the world has ever seen.

One of the traits that separates leaders from the rest is absolute **perseverance**. Life is a funny thing. Somehow, we are grown up to fear failure. In school, we are graded on a scale from A to F or E to F (in the case of New York City elementary public schools) and failure is shown to be the place that we should stay away from. We should run from it with all our might and everything in us. Supposedly, those who get the Fs are the ones who are not smart enough, don't work hard enough and don't care enough. Even if this is not stated explicitly in most educational settings, the underlying message is there because most students are afraid of receiving an F. Now, I'm not saying that they should fail intentionally. I'm simply pointing out the rap failure gets. It's not the failure that's the problem. It's the getting up and pushing forward on what you believe AFTER failing that we don't do enough of. We are not always taught how and failing is most often brought up as an experience you *don't want* to have. Failure is set up as the opposite of success when, in fact, it is actually a part of it.

"Failure is not the opposite of success. Rather, it is a part of the journey."

We often forget the failures that bring us to success because we are taught to focus on the pinnacle not the pothole. As a child, I was trying to learn how to ride a bicycle, like most kids my age. Some were learning because their parents were pushing them along on the street. Some were learning because they were alternating pedaling and falling. Me? I learned to ride in a matter of 2 hours one afternoon. I was 7 years old and somehow, I figured out the key to riding wasn't the pedaling, but the balancing. I was staying at a friend's house in Montreal, Canada, for a few days and we decided to go spend some time outside. He got out his bicycle and began wobbling up the street. I looked over at the other multi-colored banana seat bicycle in the garage and decided I was up to the challenge. Pushing the bicycle up the driveway, I remember my heart racing a bit because I hadn't done this before. You see, where I grew up before this, no one had bicycles. If you wanted to ride or move down the street without walking, you had to build your own little go-cart or street vehicle from scratch...wood, spare rubber and ingenuity. So, this was my first opportunity to actually ride a bicycle.

Up the driveway we went and my friend, Martin, began wobbling down the street. I tried to follow but quickly realized I was unable to balance without putting my leg on the ground. Of course, I couldn't pedal and use my leg as a kickstand at the same time. I was going to have to learn how to ride if I wanted to play. The adults weren't out. (This was back when kids actually played in the streets without grown-ups.) I needed to figure out how to make this riding thing happen on my own. I looked at the driveway. This driveway was about 40 feet downhill into the garage. I knew if I got into the garage, I would be safe and probably wouldn't scrape my knees like I would on the asphalt. So, I figured out that I could start at the top of the driveway and coast easily down into the garage. Somehow, when I did that, it was easier to balance. I did this over and over for an hour, after some time beginning to add in the process of pedaling. Pretty soon, I was pedaling downhill, into the garage and making turns once I got into the garage. It was a big enough garage and I was small. After a while, I decided to go out on the street. Once on the street, I took a running start beside the bicycle and then hopped on once it got going. BALANCE! YES! It happened. I was riding. One challenge. At the end of the street, there was a big hill and everyone else was going down. I coasted to the end of the flat and simply started coasting down the hill. My feet simply stayed ready to hit the brakes. As I flew down the hill, fear and bravery welled up in me at the same time and I could feel the sense of conquering. I saw the challenge. I reached the bottom of the hill, coasted for a little bit, then hit the brakes and stopped. I'd done it! I turned around to glance back at the hill and swelled up with pride at the sight of it. I'd conquered THE HILL! I was officially a rider! I saw the activity I wanted to participate in and I persevered until it happened.

Well, every kid learns how to ride a bicycle, Robert!

They do but somewhere along the way they begin to lose the perseverance factor because they begin to fear failure more. We have so many potential leaders who are trampled simply because they fell victim to the idea that failure is the end.

WAY #7 - LEADERS ARE UNDAUNTED BY FAILURE

The truth is failure builds character and is the door to further knowledge. If you are persevering and pushing through those failure experiences in your life, then you are a leader.

Let's look at you.

Discovery Questions

1. How do you feel when something you are doing flops? Excited or Bummed? Why?

2. When you encounter failure, what do you typically do next?

3. What would you list as your greatest success?

4. How many failures had you encountered before that success?

8

What's Your Label?

The word 'leader' is simply a label. We love our labels, don't we? We use them to categorize each other. We use them to fit people into understandable boxes. We use them to share personality styles and roles.

Labels are neither good nor bad. They are just tools we use to create some sense of structure in our minds. The challenge comes when we assume one size fits all or only people of a certain ilk can carry specific labels. With regard to the label of leader, we've heard that leaders are born. We've seen people assumed to be leaders simply because they are a part of a certain group or family. I've personally seen some excluded from leadership because they were not invited to be part of a certain tradition.

However, leadership is not exclusive. We all have the opportunity and possibility for leadership. In fact, I believe we all lead at some point in our lives. We may not lead a large organization, but we lead in some way. We may lead in our families. We may lead in a game played among friends. We may lead our children. We may lead because we see a need. Leadership is a trait or an activity in which we all get involved at some point. As I mentioned in Chapter 4, John Maxwell simply refers to leadership as 'influence'. If there is any point in your life at which you have influence over anyone or anything, you are leading. The challenge for many people is *leadership is scary*. Leadership means you open yourself up to criticism. It means you automatically become vulnerable to attack. A target gets placed on you and it stays with you wherever you move.

I remember one of the first times someone took the time to tell me I was a leader. I was about halfway through my sophomore year of college. I went to a small school in Massachusetts and when I got there, I looked for some opportunities to get involved with one of the things I loved most...music. During my first week, I saw a sign on one of the dormitory walls for a group looking to audition keyboard players. I saw it but I didn't do anything about it because, frankly, I didn't think I was good enough to play for a college group. I had done some playing for one of the choirs at my church back in New York, but this was a new area, a new level, and I didn't think I was ready. However, a friend of mine was going to audition and he told me to come along. When we got there, the leader of the group said he was on his way to a music store to buy a keyboard and invited us to come along. We went along and while at the store, we both played some of the keyboards. The group leader invited both of us to play for his group. This led to us both playing for the gospel choir on campus as well as several other groups. I loved doing this because it gave me the opportunity to travel a little with some of the groups as well as constantly learning new material.

"...there are some who have been equipped whether they know it or not and as much as they try to hide it, it leaks out from time to time."

One day, during my sophomore year, one of the campus chaplains saw me and called me over. I wasn't sure why he was calling me at the time but what he said during this conversation would stick with me and impact me a bit differently than any other person saying it to me. He called me over and said, "Robert, I've seen you on campus playing with these different groups and I've seen you interacting with your classmates on campus. I don't know what it is or how to explain it exactly to you. I can't really give you examples. But, there is just something telling me that you are hiding behind the keyboard when you should actually be out in front of it. Do you know what I mean?"

I swallowed quickly because my dad had mentioned many times before that he expected me to lead. Dad had this expectation because I was the first-born and he was also a leader. To me, this felt like pressure coming from my dad and I wanted no part of it. But, from the campus chaplain (his name was Jerome), it felt like I had been outed. It felt like there was a secret I had been carrying and someone from my world came to tell this guy my secret. So, my response to Jerome was, "No, I'm not exactly sure what you mean."

He continued, "Well, I'm not sure how to explain it further. But, I just want you to let this sit on your heart. There are some people who are thrust into leadership; there are some who choose to do it but never equip themselves to do it effectively; and then there are some who have been equipped whether they know it or not and as much as they try to hide it, it leaks out from time to time. You're leaking, brother!"

I went back to my dorm room unsure of what to do with it. At first, I wondered where the leak was and how I could plug it. Then I wondered what would happen if I simply opened up the hole and let it flow. At the beginning of that summer, I made the decision to start a vocal group. For me, a typically introverted (label), sometimes shy (label), quiet (label) guy, this was a huge decision. I didn't know what it would take. I wasn't sure if people thought enough of me to be a part of a group I was leading and I wasn't sure where it would go. But, that summer, I took a notebook with me everywhere and constantly jotted ideas, wrote songs and figured out how I would lead this group of people.

When school was about to begin again, I began to contact people, letting them know of my intentions and asking them to be a part. I asked 12 people and they all said yes. That was huge. Up until the writing of this chapter, I wasn't really sure why many of them said yes. So, I reached out to them, and here are some of their responses:

Tracey Richardson – *" What I do remember most was your AP-PROACH! You presented your vision to us....what "sound" you were looking for. You made us feel SPECIAL to have been "chosen".....cause soOOooo many groups at the time were being formed. You were calm & clear with the what your objective was for the group. You were ambitious ....but not anxious, or over-bearing....and you did not come across as desperate. So for me, the thing that stood out most was your approach....& how you presented this vision that you had for Simply*

His.. .....Your passion to minister was my passion to minister ...and the LOVE of singing was a major factor as well. To me....Simply His was not just gonna be ANOTHER singing group on campus......I knew that we were gonna' be "different'....and we were!"

Ruel Forbes – *"You had proven your voice and musical chops. Paid your dues and got the promotion to leadership. We had an opportunity to travel for the college as sales people too. I believe that was arranged at the outset. So add to your own skills the ability to structure an attractive deal. Hope that helps gel it down into the qualities and factors promoting your leadership."*

Ruel reminded me of something I'd forgotten. In trying to figure out how I could create something that was different, I'd pitched the idea of the group as a recruiting tool to the college's director for advancement. That allowed us to have access to some musical equipment as well as travel on behalf of the college.

Adrienne Townsend (US Navy Chaplain) – *"I believed in the vision that Robert Kennedy had and his passion for quality music ministry was contagious. He was talented and his confidence and drive attracted talent. I was honored to have the opportunity to join a group of talented musicians."*

Tracey and Adrienne both mentioned the word vision. They saw confidence and calmness. Little did they know how scared I felt inside. They didn't know the little boy inside who was constantly screaming HELP, who felt he didn't understand how the world around him worked. And yet, they placed a portion of their lives in my hands. As a leader, this is truly what happens.

People place their time, their energy, their trust, their talent, and their hope in your hands. It's up to you to ***choose courage*** in order to repay this precious gift they have entrusted to you.

9

What Happens Next?

So, what's next? Hopefully, by now you have done two things:

1. conducted a thorough evaluation of why you do what you do;
2. decided to shrug off the opinions of others in order to fully take on your leadership mantle.

Leadership is influence but the greatest leadership word is **ACTION**. What action will you take next? What do you truly believe in...so much that you will choose to take one step towards it TODAY?

There are all kinds of leaders. There are bad ones. There are good ones and there are GREAT ones. Good ones take action. GREAT ones take action and simultaneously spur others to action. They don't sit on an idea for long periods of time while trying to figure out a plan. They bring it out into the open, share a vision and empower others to co-create the plan. They step into possibility first. They move forward knowing the possibility of failure but believing the innovation will change the world. They wake up with doubts and fears but immediately open a cereal box of faith to grab a bowl.

Doubts and fears take hold in the same place leadership begins…your mind. Many ideas and visions are formed but they get snuffed out because we allow them to live in the same space as fear. Fear is a blanket whose only purpose is to snuff out fire. If we allow it to exist in the same room as the fire, sooner or later, the blanket will get over to the fire to do it's job. But, when we make the ideas and visions accessible, in other words, when we lose the criticism anxiety and begin to share them, we move them to a place where ACTION can begin.

Your first step is to *get your ideas out of your brain*. Over the course of this book, I have asked questions at the end of each chapter and suggested you write the answers in a personal notebook or paper. The intent is to encourage you towards this first step of getting the ideas out of your mind and on to a visible medium. You may want to take this further and do something like starting a blog to share your ideas, visions and concepts publicly. You may want to do what I have done here and write a book. You may want to simply begin sharing a social media status update or two. Whatever it is, make the decision to separate the ideas from where fear lives. Remember that fear is stuck. It can't exist outside of your mind. You can't touch fear. It isn't something you can see physically. Fear is desperate because it's trapped and it knows it. So, fear's job is to keep your creativity hostage. Fear tries to keep you constricted because it knows that when you become fully expressed, there is no stopping you. You are a leader and you will lead an army with your ideas. Believe the ideas were given to you for a reason.

They were not given on their own. You were equipped with the ability to move them outside of the intangible zone, through the possibility zone and into the reality zone.

Your second step is to *choose your team*. This doesn't happen on your own. This is not a race to prove you are Superman or Woman. This is a journey to create impact. It's a road where you will use your gifts to serve and make a huge difference. Get the idea out of your mind, then choose people who have different gifts to help you execute. You might be chosen to help them execute theirs. Leaders may often feel lonely, but they never work alone. They are no good on their own. Choose a team who inspires you. Choose a team who is excited about forward progress and change. Choose a team who understands purpose.

Your third step is to *decide which step you can take today* and every day. Ideas grow a little at a time. They can also explode pretty quickly. But, there are no skip days. You're a leader now. You are creating the destination and mastering the map. It's time to take consistent ownership. It's time to ACT!

After you have completed this book, I hope you will be inspired and fired up to **STEP IN** to your leadership place. If you are already leading, I hope you will **STEP UP** your leadership pace. I really hope you will understand leadership is not a race. But a journey where you should take some time to **LAUGH** out loud, **LIVE** your best life and **LEAD** WITH PURPOSE!

Acknowledgments

Nothing is ever accomplished solo. There are always people who help make the engine run. Some of them are asked or hired. And there are others who simply show their love by doing without even being asked. Thank you.

I wanted to specifically acknowledge:

Chris Edmonds – thanks for the gift edits and your friendship which requires no quid pro quo.

Lael Caesar – your keen eye makes me better and bolder.

George Watson – I'll never forget.

Pamela Slim – you have no idea how much it means to watch your heart in action.

Jerome Spears – you may never know the true impact of your words. Thank you.

Robert Wallace – your mentorship has been meaningful even when you didn't say a word.

Lois Peters – kindness oozes from your pores and I'm blessed to be a recipient. Thank you.

My clients – each of you has taught me to be a better coach, speaker, trainer and leader. I treasure every moment. Thank you.

About The Author

Robert Kennedy III is an entrepreneur, keynote speaker, trainer and author. A former classroom teacher, he currently hosts the Leading With Purpose Podcast. In 2002, he started his first business, an online music promotion portal which reached #3 most visited nationally for its industry.

Robert's first book was a technical software manual, **The Articulate Studio Cookbook**, coming from his time as a trainer for online learning development. His second book, *28 Days To A New Me: A Journey of Commitment*, was his first entry into the personal development arena.

Currently, he works with corporations on leadership and communication strategies and contributes to publications such Huffington Post.

Learn more about him online at www.robertkennedy3.com. Follow him as @robertkennedy3 on Twitter, Instagram and Facebook.

Broken Rules

You thought you were done, didn't you? Every time I write a book, I look at the formatting information. They tell you to include the Table of Contents, Body Matter, Preface, Foreword, Resources...not necessarily in that order. But, while systems are good, I've gotten to the place in life where I'm learning that sometimes, just sometimes, it's good to insert your own rule.

Each of us, from birth, is inducted into a life of systems, telling us we should do things a certain way. It's not until later on that we figure out we actually have options and can make choices. So, we follow the rules until figure out we can sometimes create our own.

In this case, I'm creating my own rule. I'm continuing to write after the book is done because...well, I can. You see, in order to challenge the status quo, *sometimes leaders are rule breakers.* They might not break the law of the state. However, they may break the little unspoken rules we are expected to follow. And whether people admit it or not, this is the spunk which causes others to follow. Many people do this because they often wish they could summon the audacity to do so themselves.

Here's the real end. Go, be audacious! **Be bold!** Take the lead and sometimes, break a rule.

www.ingramcontent.com/pod-product-compliance
Lightning Source LLC
Chambersburg PA
CBHW070358190526
45169CB00003B/1040